LONDON MIDLAND STEAM on the ex-L & Y

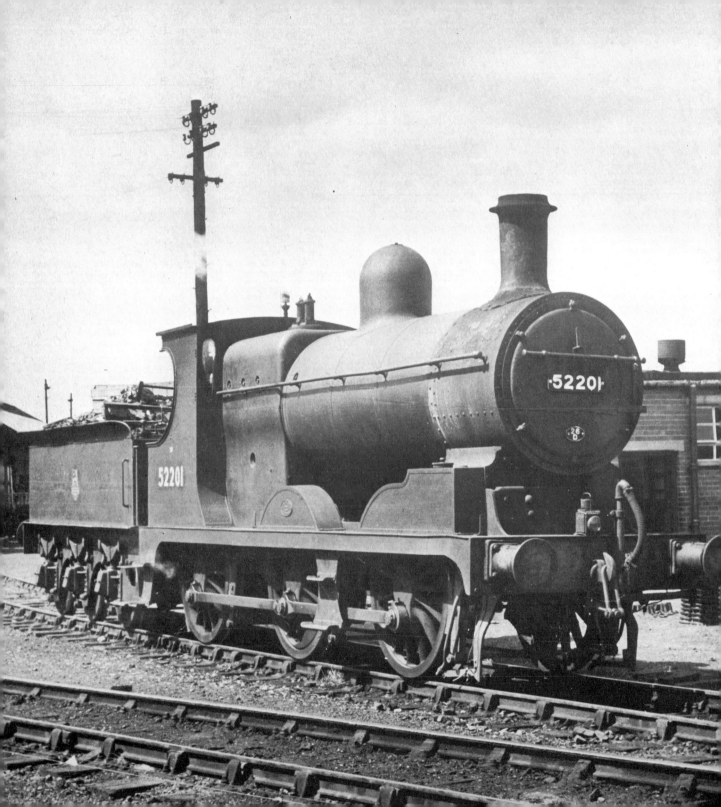

LONDON MIDLAND STEAM ON THE EX-L&Y

R. S. GREENWOOD

D. BRADFORD BARTON LIMITED

Frontispiece: Lancashire & Yorkshire Railway ''A'' Class 0-6-0 No. 52201, a rebuild with saturated Belpaire firebox, simmers in the sunshine in May 1959 at Castleton Central Materials Depot.

© *copyright D. Bradford Barton 1975*   *ISBN 0 85153 231 4*

printed and bound in Great Britain by Mackays of Chatham PLC

for the publishers

D. BRADFORD BARTON LTD · Trethellan House · Truro · Cornwall · England

introduction

The Lancashire & Yorkshire Railway spread itself for some 600 miles across the two Counties of the Red and White Rose. Much of this way it ran through industrial areas where the typical backdrop was angular cotton mills, stone quarries and colliery spoilheaps, although in the Pennines hill scenery alternates with the drab industrial scene.

So densely populated was—and is—the area traversed by the Railway that the line had a higher proportion of signals and signalboxes per mile of track than any other major British railway. Stations serving large towns follow closely together, so that long non-stop runs for passenger trains were rare.

From the early years of this century, when pioneering schemes in electrification, fitted freight and block trains were introduced, the formation of the LMSR, and then British Railways, brought a general lowering of standards to the common denominator of the larger railway. Many of the L & Y passenger services were decelerated and rationalisation led to the withdrawal of the Liverpool–Newcastle and Liverpool–Hull trains in favour of the LNWR and CLC routes. Otherwise little effect of the changes of 1923 and 1948 could be seen on the passenger trains. These continued to run on the same routes, often in paths that had remained unchanged for 70 years or more, and no attempt was made to view either county as a homogeneous whole and to organise an integrated service.

The pattern of freight traffic changed more when the smaller depots closed and, later, even depots serving large towns. The staple traffic was coal and as the Lancashire coalfield declined, more and more came westwards through the Pennines from Yorkshire. Raw cotton from the docks was an early casualty and specialised types of traffic such as fish from Fleetwood and Hull, vegetables for Oldham Road, or pigeon specials, were all terminated.

To the end of steam, former L & Y depots remained

responsible for working the bulk of the traffic on L & Y metals. 'Foreign' engines frequently appeared but rarely on a scheduled basis. In the West Riding the LNWR depot at Hillhouse and the Midland one at Normanton worked a lot of the local passenger traffic, leaving the L & Y sheds at Mirfield and Wakefield to concentrate on freight.

The general scene was one of frequent trains, long coal trains, even longer returning empties, a host of parcels trains in the evening, well-used goods loops and busy junctions.

The photographers whose work is included in this volume are W. H. Ashcroft, Dr. J. G. Blears, A. J. Cocker, J. A. Cox, D. Greenwood, R. S. Greenwood, Barry Hilton, Brian Hilton, I. G. Holt, P. Hutchinson, G. W. Morrison, K. Roberts and the Rt. Rev. Eric Treacy.

The book is broadly divided into the following subjects: main line services; Yorkshire locals; Manchester and the Residentials; Liverpool; Horwich; Freight power; L & Y locomotives; Pugs; Todmorden; Summit Tunnel; the Oldham branch; Rochdale; Bury; Bolton; Southport; Blackburn; Accrington; the Scotswood—Red Bank ECS; and excursions.

The editorial proceeds from this volume are being used to assist the 'L & Y Saddletanks Fund' in the task of preserving their three locomotives and one coach.

The only Restaurant Car train over the ex-L & Y main line in British Railways days was the 10.30 a.m. Liverpool (Exchange)–Newcastle and return. 'Jubilee' No. 45698 *Mars* was one of a trio of engines of this class at Bank Hall shed in Liverpool regularly employed on the working. In November 1958, No. 45698 still retained the small straight-sided tender as it set out from Sowerby Bridge heading towards Brighouse.

The 10.30 a.m. was cut back to York and its restaurant car removed when the 'Trans-Pennine' services were introduced over the rival ex-LNWR route at the end of 1960. Passenger trains on the ex-L & Y route were dieselised on 1 January 1962. A few days before this, at the start of the Christmas holidays on 23 December 1961, No. 45698 *Mars* takes advantage of the level stretch past Smithy Bridge between Rochdale and Littleborough to get the 10.30 a.m. up to speed. The V2 2-6-2 No. 60877 waiting in the Goods Loop is a stranger. Because of their heavy axleloading, the LMR restricted visits of these engines west of the Pennines to one trip a day over the LNWR/CLC route to Liverpool but when the return working was cancelled the engine had to make its way back as best it could.

From 1958 to 1960, a single unrebuilt 'Patriot', No. 45517, working from Bank Hall shed, was a frequent sight on the Liverpool–Newcastle express and it is seen here emerging from Elland Tunnel in February 1960. Passenger services over the ex-L & Y line from Sowerby Bridge to Wakefield and York ceased in 1970, and summer holiday trains are now the only change from freight trains through Elland.

The Manchester area shed which provided motive power for the main line turns into Yorkshire was Agecroft and a fleet of 'Black Fives' handled more than half of the York diagrams. On Saturdays in winter, two of these Agecroft 4-6-0s would doublehead the 2.07 p.m. from York. In this photograph Nos. 45338 and 45337 await the rightaway from Rochdale.

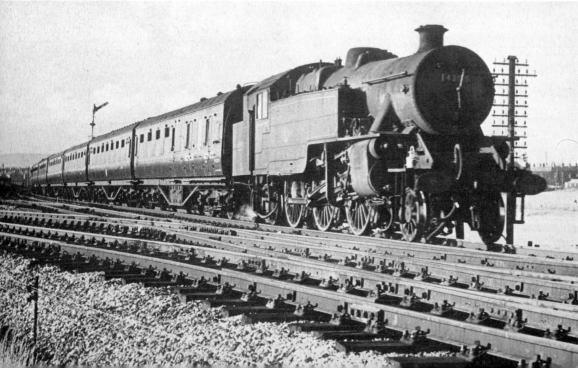

The fastest schedule between Wakefield and Manchester was accorded to the 5.15 p.m. from York, a train that changed engines at Wakefield. Sowerby Bridge shed provided the motive power for the second leg of the journey, although it had nothing larger than Fairburn Class 4 2-6-4 tanks. On occasions at weekends in summer this train loaded to thirteen coaches and serious loss of time was inevitable. The normal loading, however, was seven bogies, as on this occasion in July 1960 as No. 42150 passes Castleton South Junction.

The trains from Liverpool or Southport in the west and Bradford and Leeds (Central) in the east were more important than the York trains in terms of numbers of passengers carried. Formed of two portions, 'Bradford in front, Leeds in rear', they were divided eastbound at Low Moor and joined together westbound at Halifax. One of Bank Hall's Caprotti 4-6-0s, No. 44744, heads out of Halifax amidst scenery very typical of the area, with the 5.10 p.m. from Leeds in July 1961. Three Caprotti engines came to Bank Hall depot in 1958 from the Bristol area. It took the local crews some time to master their peculiarities on gradients—particularly the steep climb out of Manchester (Victoria) to Newton Heath.

For a long time Bank Hall shed had no conventional 'Black Fives' on its allocation and the unique member of the class fitted with outside Stephenson link motion, No. 44767, spent most of its working life there. Originally fitted with a double chimney and electric lighting, these refinements had been removed by the winter of 1960. Platelayers engaged on fishplate greasing step back as it leaves Rochdale with the 12.30 p.m. from Liverpool (Exchange) to Leeds.

Displaced by diesels on the Settle–Carlisle line, a few rebuilt 'Royal Scots' formerly allocated to Holbeck spent a few weeks in the autumn of 1961 at Low Moor shed. Prior to this Low Moor boasted only 'Black Fives' for its passenger trains although a couple of 'Jubilees' were to be allocated there later for excursion work. Since they were too wide for the Liverpool line from Wigan (Wallgate), the 'Royal Scots' were confined to a slow return trip between Bradford and Southport, on which No. 46130 *The West Yorkshire Regiment* is seen engaged on one sunny September morning. By the beginning of November, the 'Royal Scots' had moved on to Mirfield, where they were employed on freight work until their early withdrawal.

The Leeds portions avoided Bradford by taking the spur from Bowling Junction to Laisterdyke. Stanier Class 4 2-6-4T No. 42644 takes the Leeds coaches off an extra from Blackpool in 1966, the preceding Bradford portion having already descended the steep incline in the foreground which leads directly into Exchange station.

'Patriot' No. 45517, making a change from the Newcastle train, by this time working the 1.15 p.m. Bradford–Liverpool Exchange express, passes ex-L M S 2P 4-4-0 No. 40588 at Castleton on the 12.42 p.m. Liverpool–Rochdale slow.

Walsden station—situated at the eastern end of Winterbutlee Tunnel and with low platforms and wooden steps to assist passengers board the trains—was an old-fashioned survival. Its booking office was in the end building of a terrace of houses. Less than a month after this photograph of Standard Class 4 4-6-0 No. 75017 on the 4.37 p.m. Manchester–Halifax was taken in July 1961, the station was closed. An engine of this type from Southport shed was the invariable motive power for this train on weekdays. All the Southport workings seemed to be tightly rostered and their engines rarely strayed off the booked turns.

'Crab' 2-6-0s from Agecroft and Newton Heath sheds handled much of the local passenger traffic in the Calder Valley on a regular basis all the year round. Other Divisions may have regarded them as freight engines but they were very much mixed traffic machines on the former L & Y lines. No. 42725 leaves Greetland in July 1959 with an evening Wakefield–Manchester stopping train.

Also at Greetland in July 1959, Stanier 2-6-2T No. 40140—one of a small batch at Sowerby Bridge shed—pulls out with a Normanton to Sowerby Bridge local. Only a few ex-L & Y sheds had engines of this class allocated to them but the class were overhauled at Horwich Works and examples from as far afield as Tredegar in South Wales could therefore be seen whilst running-in.

The line from Wakefield and York joins the line from Leeds and Bradford at Milner Royd Junction, a short distance east of Sowerby Bridge station—a high-speed junction with movable blades on the diamond crossing. The narrow tender fitted to the class is perhaps an asset to tender-first-running as 'Crab' No. 42890 heads the 4.42 p.m. Halifax–Manchester train on 6 July 1961.

Another class of 2-6-0, the Ivatt Class 4MT, was regularly seen on the 9.05 a.m. Manchester–Wakefield, the engine having previously worked up on the early morning Normanton Mail. In May 1961, No. 43074 of Normanton shed overtakes ex-LNWR 0-8-0 No. 49034 in the loop at Castleton South Junction.

Many of the Yorkshire local trains were powered by Fowler Class 4 2-6-4Ts, including a number working from the ex-LNWR shed at Hillhouse, Huddersfield. Here No. 42413, with an evening Bradford–Penistone (via Halifax) local, rounds the curve at the foot of the steep incline from Dryclough Junction, Halifax, and joins the main Wakefield line at Greetland station. A short distance further on the train will branch off the main line at Bradley Wood towards Huddersfield.

Later the same day, sister engine No. 42310, one of the earlier batch built without cab side windows, enters Lightcliffe station between Bradford and Halifax on a similar working. This was one of the three routes between Bradford and Huddersfield—the others were via the Spen Valley and via Bailiff Bridge.

Engines in store at Sowerby Bridge shed for the winter in February 1960 included Stanier Class 3 2-6-2Ts Nos. 40147 and 40190, and Fowler Class 4 2-6-4Ts Nos. 42380 and 42411.

An overhead view
of Agecroft Class 5
4-6-0 No. 44823 on
a midday Wakefield
to Manchester slow
about to plunge
into Sowerby Bridge
Tunnel. The shed
lies to the left of the
line, with the goods
yard off to the
right. The town
itself, hemmed in at
the bottom of the
valley, is dominated
by mill chimneys
so typical of the
Yorkshire woollen
district.

Stanier Class 4
2-6-4 tank engines
worked over all
sections of the old
L & Y and Bolton was
a particularly good
place to see them;
Nos. 42626, 42630
and 42653 take a
mid-morning break
behind the down
platform adjacent
to the raised
signalbox in May
1961.

24

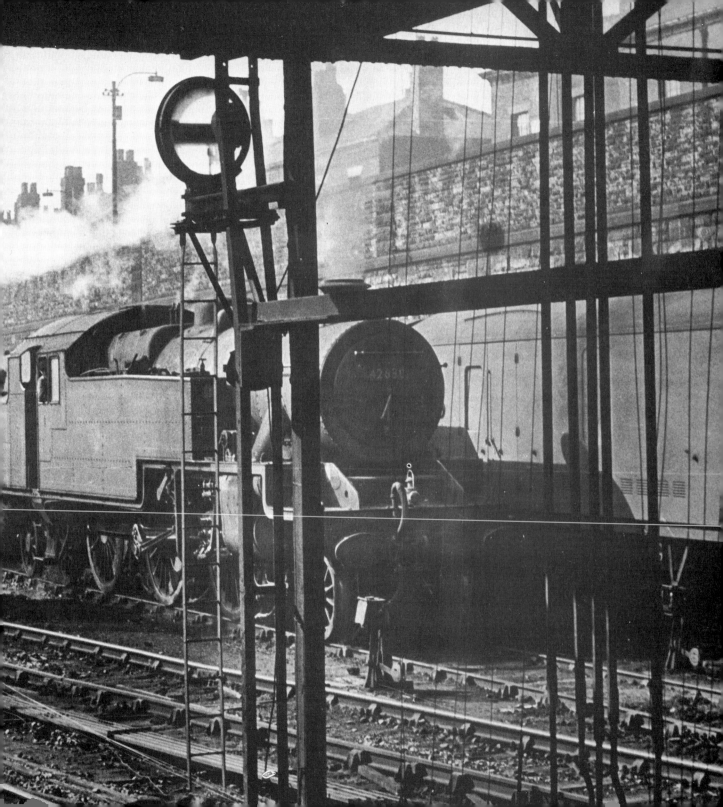

Manchester (Victoria) was the headquarters of the old L & Y, housing the administrative offices as well as being the largest and busiest station. In the station as rebuilt in 1903, Platforms 1 to 10 and 17 were east-facing bays, Platform 11 was a common platform extended via 'No. 11 middle' into the LNWR Exchange station and Nos. 12 to 16 were the through lines. The 'Bays' pilot invariably stood in front of the Turntable Signalbox, named after the turntable that once stood just off the platform end for the use of engines on the local passenger services making a quick turnround. The duty found regular employment for one of Newton Heath's 'Breadvans', in this case No. 40063. These engines had a very chequered career on ex L & Y metals and it was said that only Bacup men could make them run satisfactorily.

In the late afternoon a procession of residential trains left Manchester bound for the coast. All of them started either at the carriage sidings at Cheetham Hill (above) where two 'Black Fives' stand ready on their trains as a 4F 0-6-0 runs down light engine, or at Queens Road (below) with Class 5 No. 45233 drawing out of the sidings, whilst the double chimney 'Jubilee' No. 45596 *Bahamas* is still making up its fire.

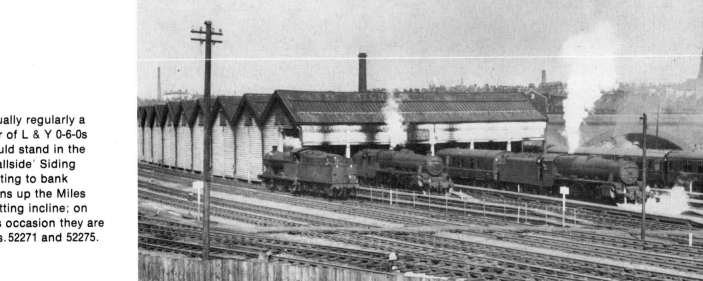

qually regularly a air of L & Y 0-6-0s ould stand in the Vallside' Siding aiting to bank ains up the Miles atting incline; on is occasion they are os. 52271 and 52275.

28

The heavier trains to Blackpool were usually entrusted to 'Jubilees'. One of the seaside allocation, No. 45574 *India*, stands at Platform 5 in Preston station on 4 May 1959 with an express from Manchester.

any of the lighter Blackpool and Southport residential trains from Manchester and the other cotton towns were rked by Compound 4-4-0s. One washing day in 1953 No. 41193, with a Manchester–Blackpool express (above), uts off steam at Eatocks Colliery Sidings box on the Atherton line, ready to branch north over the Dobbs Brow ur towards Chorley and so avoid the congestion at Bolton. Sister engine No. 41102 (below) blows off as it enters eston station with the 4.35 p.m. Rochdale–Blackpool (Central) in July 1957.

Five years later, the same engine, with large Stanier-pattern tender, slowly rounds the curve from Chorley to join the West Coast main line at Euxton Junction on a Saturday Manchester–Blackpool train. The short stretch of the West Coast main line from Euxton Junction to Preston was jointly owned by the L & Y and the LNWR.

A Blackpool to Liverpool (Exchange) train in pre-war days leaving Preston behind Compound No. 1192. In business and financial terms Liverpool was no less important than Manchester. Despite the close proximity of Southport and the other seaside towns served by the pioneer electrified line, there was a well-patronised service from Liverpool to Blackpool.

Ormskirk marked the outer end of electrification on the line from Liverpool in the Preston direction. An electric local train stands in the bay there as Class 5 No. 45464 pauses on a train from Blackpool (above). Drifting into Ormskirk from the south with a Liverpool–Preston semifast (note the class 'A' headcode despite the non-corridor stock) is Standard Class 2 2-6-0 No. 78037 (below). A small batch of engines of this class at Bank Hall shed did a lot of spirited running on the lighter trains on this and other services from Liverpool (Exchange).

Besides the Standard Class 2 2-6-0s, Bank Hall had a stud of Standard Class 4 4-6-0s, Nos. 75045-9. These were later to be joined by others as well. The Class 4s had replaced Bank Hall's Compounds on most of the local work but from time to time had to take a turn to Bradford and back with an express when the shed's resources were hard pressed. No. 75046 approaches Walton Junction station in the Liverpool suburbs with an afternoon train for Preston in May 1965.

The site chosen for the new main L & Y workshops in the 1880s, to replace the original facilities at Miles Platting and Bury, was at Horwich, which was served by a short branch line from Blackrod on the Bolton–Chorley line. Stanier Class 4 2-6-4T No. 42561 waits at the single platform terminus with a Saturday lunchtime train for Bolton.

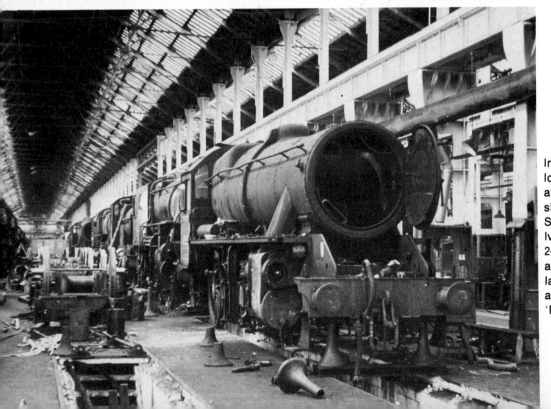

In February 1962, locomotives receiving attention in the erecting shop at Horwich included Stanier 2-6-0 No. 42953, Ivatt and Standard Class 4 2-6-0s, 'Crabs', 4F 0-6-0s and Stanier 8F 2-8-0s. The last L & Y engine to receive attention there was a 'Pug', No. 51218, in 1963.

Later to be preserved at Clapham and then York in a decorative but inaccurate livery, *Wren*, one of the narrow-gauge Works shunters, is here in its normal habitat on 9 August 1953. Note the wartime camouflage still visible on the walls and roofs of the buildings.

Works shunting was carried out by a batch of L & Y 0-6-0 saddle tanks. Five of these engines in Departmental Stock retained their old LMS numbers until withdrawal, although other members of the class used as Works shunters at Crewe were numbered in the running series. Nos. 11305 and 11368 display the contrasting styles of smokebox door; the former has the original type with central dart, the latter the Hughes modification.

Running-in after overhaul at Horwich: Stanier 2-6-0 No.42945 on a Bolton–Leeds
passenger working, and 4F 0-6-0 No.44247 (below) on empty stock ready for a day
excursion from Littleborough to Blackpool.

Important though the passenger traffic might be, freight was the mainstay on the ex-L & Y lines. After 1948 the
whole class of Fowler 7F 0-8-0s, 175 strong, gravitated here to replace the older L & Y eight-coupled machines.
No.49618, one of the last Fowler survivors, passes Castleton station with a short freight from Brewery Sidings
(Miles Platting) to Royton Junction in May 1960.

The Fowler engines were themselves in turn rapidly displaced by 'WD' 2-8-0s. All the ex-L & Y sheds handling freight traffic had large allocations of these, the largest number naturally being at Wakefield. No. 90561 climbs the last few chains to Summit Tunnel on 1 January 1962 with an empty wagon train from Middleton Junction to the Yorkshire coalfield.

Stanier 8F 2-8-0s were comparative rarities on the L & Y section until the early 1960's, when they quickly infiltrated to replace the 'WD' 2-8-0s. Three 'Midland Eights', as Lanky enginemen described them, line up at Agecroft shed on 5 March 1966: Nos. 48714, 48224 and 48536.

Some of the ex-LNWR 7F 0-8-0s which outlived their more modern Fowler counterparts worked on to the section from LNW sheds. No. 49199, of Patricroft, rouses the echoes at Jubilee Crossing between New Hey and Shaw & Crompton on a freight bound for Royton Junction. The large marshalling yard at Royton Junction was used as a classification yard for wagons awaiting repair or scrapping. Long trains of empty wagons were regularly worked there only to be sent out again a few days later after inspection.

As the staple freight was coal traffic, fitted freights were few in number and consequently Class 5 4-6-0s were not often seen on this type of work until the last two or three years of steam traction. Making an all-out assault on Hoghton Bank between Preston and Blackburn is No. 44819 in March 1966.

Most shunting and local freight work in the area in later years was handled by Class 2 2-6-0s such as No. 46417, heading for Littleborough on the daily trip work

Ex-L & Y 0-6-0ST
No. 51497 leaving
Royton Junction on
the evening of
12 June 1958 with
the 8.35 p.m. freight
from Hartford
Sidings, Oldham, to
Moston.

43

A number of the 'A' class 0-6-0s were rebuilt by George Hughes with Belpaire fireboxes although retaining saturated boilers; No. 52161, a Southport engine, has just arrived at Horwich Works in March 1958.

The typical freight from an engine shed: empty wooden loco coal wagons and a steel-bodied mine wagon full of ash set out from Lower Darwen shed in July 1952 bound for Bolton in charge of L & Y Class No. 52399.

Other 'A' class engines had
superheated boilers, some as
rebuilds whilst the rest were
built new in that condition.
No. 52619, seen at Preston in
August 1951, was one of those
rebuilt as superheated engines.
Many of the ex-L & Y 0-6-0s and
2-4-2Ts went to former LNW
sheds after the 1923
amalgamation, being somewhat
of an improvement on the
antiquated Webb machines that
monopolised those places.

The Hughes Railmotors also
travelled further afield after the
Grouping, but the last one in
traffic was No. 10617 which
lasted until March 1948 on the
shuttle service between
Blackrod and Horwich.

When first built as L & Y No. 826 in 1909, B R No. 52526 was one of the first classes of superheated engines built in the country. During L M S days however this pioneer was downgraded and provided with a saturated boiler, the only outward distinguishing feature being the manner in which the front sand-boxes projected beyond the smokebox front. No. 52526 is seen on a short coal working to Castleton Sidings in 1960.

The L & Y Radial 2-4-2 passenger tanks came in various guises; No. 50850 working as additional station pilot at Southport during the annual August Flower Show in 1961 has a saturated Belpaire boiler and long bunker. Behind the engine can be seen an electric train for Crossens, a service abandoned shortly after this date.

Push-pull-fitted No. 50648, working 'The Dolly Tub Express' between Radcliffe (Central) and Bolton, has the roundtop firebox, short bunker and extended coal rails. No. 50651 (below), similar except for the Belpaire firebox, is employed on the last day of the Bury to Holcombe Brook passenger services on 4 May 1952. This branch was first electrified in 1913 with overhead collection, and was later converted to 1200v d.c. third-rail to allow through running with Manchester–Bury electrics. Steam traction returned for the last few months of passenger operations after the electric equipment became life-expired.

In pre-war days, No. 10412, which was one of the original Hughes saturated 4-6-0s completely rebuilt in 1921, is in LMS red livery as it heads south from Preston with a Fleetwood–Manchester train. No. 10412 was the only rebuilt engine of the class to last into BR days. Note the L & Y fishvan at the head of the train.

The last Hughes 4-6-0 to survive in service, No. 50455, was built new in 1924 with all the 1921 improvements. Most of the class had already been withdrawn before the real cure for their enormous coal consumption was found in the late 1930's. The last ten examples spent their final decade working from Blackpool shed and the last survivor made its farewell trip on 1 July 1951 with a special from Blackpool to York and back.

Another last survivor, Barton-Wright Class 2F 0-6-0 No. 52044, was kept on at Wakefield specially to shunt in certain colliery sidings at Dart[e] on the Barnsley branch. Almo[st] as if they were ashamed to ow[n] it, British Railways never had their name or coat of arms applied to this engine even though it remained in service until 1958.

After withdrawal from service, No. 52044 was purchased for preservation by Tony Cox and a minimum amount of work was done on it at Horwich Works in the summer of 1960. In particular the original style of smokebox door was substituted for the later type it had carried for the previous four or five years.

ew Bailey Yard at Salford—
med after the prison formerly
ccupying this site—was one
the haunts of 'Pug'
4-0STs. Dwarfed by modern
fice blocks and flanked by
cammell tractors as well as a
ntinental ferryvan, No. 51207
gotiates one of the many
ht curves on the sidings here.

enable the New Bailey Yard
gines to stay away from their
me shed (Agecroft) for a
ll week at a time, a coaling
age and watering facilities
ere on hand in the adjacent
alford low level yard—as
ey were at many L & Y Goods
ards. No. 51207 and 'Jinty'
6-0T No. 47631 stand at the
age as the crews take lunch.

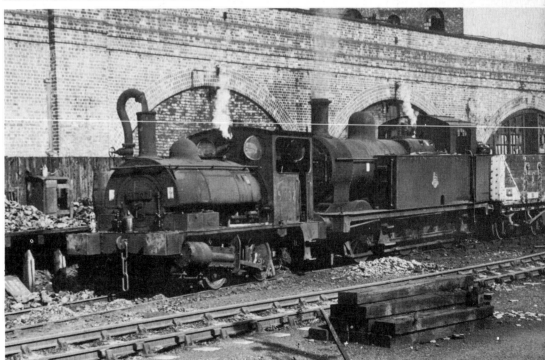

To get into New Bailey Yard, trains had to cross Irwell Street under the protection of a flagman. During a spell of duty at Preston LNW shed, No. 51204 received a shortened chimney and cut down cab—probably making it the smallest standard gauge engine on BR!

Lined up at the coaling stage at Bank Hall are BR Standard Class 6P Pacific No. 72006 *Clan Mackenzie* and 'Pug' No. 51232. The largest allocation of 'Pugs' was in the Liverpool area, for shunting duties in the Docks. To eliminate lengthy light engine runs for these diminutive engines many were shedded at the passenger shed at Bank Hall which was adjacent to several of the Dock yards and warehouses where the Pugs worked. Those based at the freight shed at Aintree worked in the yards further north along the waterfront away from Pier Head.

Todmorden, right in the heart of the Pennines, was the meeting point of three valleys cut by ice-age glaciers and boasted a busy triangular railway layout. Todmorden station lies to the west: although the signalbox at the western end of the triangle was known as Todmorden East. In L & Y days there had been another station, Stansfield Hall, at the northern end on the Burnley line. Class 5 No. 45205 rounds the curve betweenm Stansfield Hall and Hall Royd Junction at the eastern end one Saturday morning in 1962 with an empty wagon train.

On 28 December 1960, in the days when the station nameboard still advertised a passenger service over the Copy Pit line to East Lancashire, Fowler Class 4F No. 44570 enters Todmorden station with the 9.05 a.m. Manchester–Wakefield.

Patricroft 'Jubilee' No. 45558 *Manitoba* pauses with a summer Llandudno–Bradford extra, seen from the same viewpoint but looking in the opposite direction. Alongside is a Cravens d.m.u., just arrived from Accrington, which will reverse out and shunt into the bay on the left ready for departure.

st of the Copy Pit branch trains ran out of the bay platform on the right. As the junction was on a embankment, a movable scotch was used to protect the main line rather than the more usual points. Working a Mytholmroyd–Moston coal train in August 1960 is 'Jubilee' No. 45710 *Irresistible;* was a regular return working off the 7.15 a.m. Manchester–Bradford passenger train.

An empty wagon train stretching away into the distance slowly rumbles along the down goods loop from Todmorden East to Hall Royd Junction behind 'WD' 2-8-0 No.90470. In the background a 'Crab' 2-6-0 awaits its next spell of banking up to Copy Pit.

In the heart of the Calder Valley between Hebden Bridge and Todmorden, Stanier Class 8F 2-8-0 No. 48696 accelerates a summer Sheffield–Blackpool train away from the Charlestown curve speed restriction. No. 48696 was one of the class specially balanced for fast freight and passenger work, indicated by a star on the cabside. These engines were widely used on excursion trains although their lack of steam heating gear restricted their appearances to midsummer.

When, in the 1830's, George Stephenson surveyed the route for the first railway to cross the Pennines, he took the line—the Manchester and Leeds—through the Summit Gap. This entailed the construction of a tunnel, 1¾ miles in length, then the longest in the world. The valley sides appear to close in on 'WD' 2-8-0 No. 90136—blowing off even after 35 miles of continuous climbing—on a Healey Mills to Phillips Park freight which is about to plunge into the eastern portal of Summit Tunnel.

Bleak moorland and rugged stone buildings flank the line at the western end of the tunnel. A type of engine rarely seen on this line, Ivatt Class 2 2-6-2T No. 41250, heads an evening parcels train from Bradford into Lancashire.

Oldham was a considerable manufacturing centre, meriting a connection to the main line by 1845. However, its elevated position brought operating problems. The first route into the town was up the Werneth Incline, a rope-worked stretch from Middleton (originally Oldham) Junction with a gradient of 1 in 27 for just under a mile. Although rope haulage was later abandoned, a comparatively easier route—yet still with gradients of the order of 1 in 60—was opened via Hollinwood in 1880. Ex-L & Y 2-4-2T No. 50850 brings an Enthusiasts' Special up the Incline from Middleton Junction into Werneth station in 1960 with rear-end assistance from 'A' Class 0-6-0 No. 52271. The Hollinwood line can be seen trailing in from the left.

Another enthusiasts' trip, this time by brakevan, one snowy day in March 1965 with 'Jinty' 0-6-0T No. 47656 on the trip working to Higginshaw Gas Works sidings heading through the branch platforms at Royton Junction.

Beyond Oldham and towards Rochdale the line entered open scenery for a time. On 4 July 1958, during the last week of steam operation, Stanier 2-6-4T No. 42652 works the 5.25 p.m. Rochdale–Werneth passenger.

Steep gradients meant that all down excursion trains routed via Hollinwood had to be doubleheaded. The local 'Wakes' or Holiday Weeks produced as many as thirty extra trains which travelled outward one weekend and returned the next. A special from Llandudno approaches Shaw & Crompton behind ex-L & Y 'A' Class No. 52431 and Class 5 No. 45390 on 23 August 1958.

Derby Class 4F 0-6-0 No. 44214 pilots 'Jubilee' No. 45642 *Boscawen* on a Blackpool-bound special—composed entirely of non-corridor stock—in June 1962, seen appropriately enough at Jubilee Crossing, Shaw.

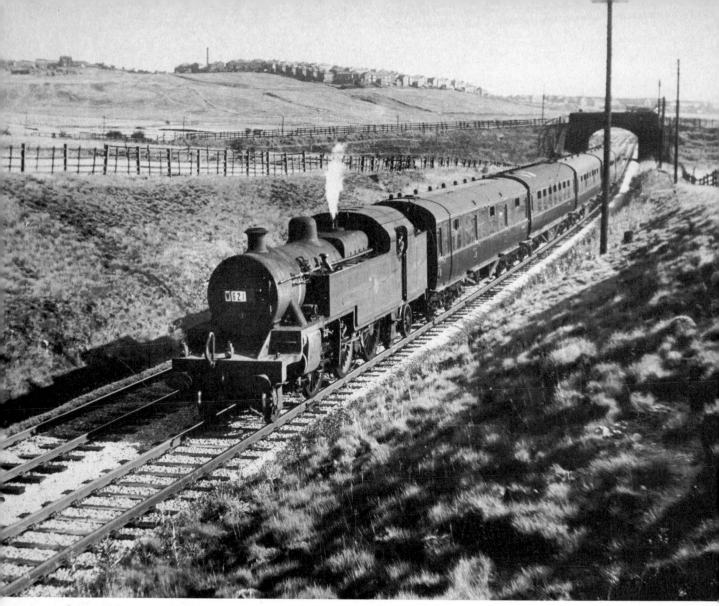

Some of the returning holiday trains from the South were routed into Oldham via the Oldham, Ashton & Guide Bridge Junction Railway (formerly LNWR/GCR joint ownership) from Stockport. Fowler 2-6-4T No. 42343 is seen at Heyside with the empty stock off such a working.

The gradients in the up direction were less severe and doubleheading was nowhere near as common. Amid scenery composed primarily of mills and warehouses, Caprotti Class 5 No. 44742 passes Shaw & Crompton station with a Liverpool–Oldham football special in February 1962.

Arriving at Rochdale East Junction, where the pilot will be detached to return light to Manchester via the main line, is an excursion for Morecambe on Whit Monday 1960. Motive power is two Newton Heath Class Fives, Nos. 45220 and 44697, the latter being paired with a self-weighing tender.

Local crews were masters of firing. Clean chimneys were the usual order of the day and black sr was uncommon. By way of contrast, No. 45232 does its worst to blot out New Hey station on an e stock train bound for Oldham.

George Hughes' last and most successful design, the 'Crabs' or 'Horwich Moguls', dominated holiday and excursion traffic in the North West. No. 42748, a Gorton engine, 'borrowed' by a North Eastern Region shed for the day, approaches Castleton with a Bank Holiday excursion for Blackpool from the South Yorkshire area.

73

A batch of superannuated ex-MR Class 3F 0-6-0s, displaced from their native haunts by diesels, arrived in 1961 at Rose Grove shed at Burnley. Thoroughly unwelcome on the L & Y, they saw very little work but on 17 July No. 43734 worked the 8.0 p.m. Rochdale–Oldham–Stoke parcels.

'Crabs', this time at Rochdale: No. 42728 on a Saturday evening excursion from Oldham to Blackpool, having piloted round the branch by Fowler Class 3 2-6-2T No. 40015, and (below) No. 42783, of Chester shed, on the ner Saturday Bradford–Llandudno train whilst No. 42702, of Manningham, is well off its beaten track with the a.m. 'all stations' from Rochdale to Liverpool. On the extreme right is Standard Class 4 No. 75016 on the a.m. fast to Southport.

Class 2P 4-4-0s remained active on semifast trains between Liverpool and Rochdale until the summer of 1961, including No. 40684 seen approaching Castleton in May of that year with the 8.40 a.m. to Liverpool. The mailvans at the rear of the train are the 'Normanton Mail' and usually went forward to Bolton by an earlier service.

By 1973 the dozen or so tracks under the bridge at the eastern approach to Bury (Knowsley Street) had been reduced to one, which carries only one coal train a day to Rawtenstall. In 1960 it was a much-busier place, even on a Sunday, as a 9F 2-10-0 headed a Sheffield to Blackpool day excursion.

On the East Lancs. section, Stanier Class 4 2-6-4T No.42646 works a late evening holiday train returning to Accrington past Bury shed at Buckley Wells over the electric line in July 1960. Beyond the engines in the shed yard on the left are the Bury Electric Car Shops and on the right can be seen electric multiple units in the holding sidings.

owsley Street, on the line running east–west, was Bury's Lancashire & Yorkshire Railway station ilst Bury (Bolton Street), on the north-south line, was the East Lancashire Railway headquarters. ey were connected by a short, steeply-graded spur which is here about to be negotiated by 'WD' .90556 and a 4F 0-6-0 heading a transfer freight for the East Lancashire section in August 1964.

The four-coach Manchester portion of a train from Glasgow, detached from the Liverpool portion at Preston, leaves Bolton (Trinity Street) in charge of rebuilt 'Patriot' No. 45540, *Sir Robert Turnbull*.

One of the few places on the former L & Y territory where Ivatt Class 2 2-6-2Ts worked on passenger duties Southport—on the 'Ormskirk Motor'—a name that was a hangover from the days when this was worked L & Y Railmotor set. No. 41277 enters Chapel Street station in August 1961.

Line-up of trains at Southport (Chapel Street) station. Standard Class 4 4-6-0 No. 75018 (Nos. 75015-9 spent most of their working life at Southport) on the 4.0 p.m. express to Manchester; 'B1' Class No. 61008 *Kudu* (one of five sent to Agecroft shed from the GC line in exchange for 'Black Fives' and thereafter kept permanently on secondary duties) with the 4.25 p.m. slow to Manchester and Fairburn 2-6-4T No. 42063 on the 4.12 p.m. for Preston.

Low Moor Class 5 No. 44695 sets out from Southport with the 1.15 p.m. express to Bradford and Leeds via Manchester on 24 August 1961. When diesel multiple units took over the Calder Valley main line in January 1962, the two daily direct trains between Southport and the West Riding were withdrawn.

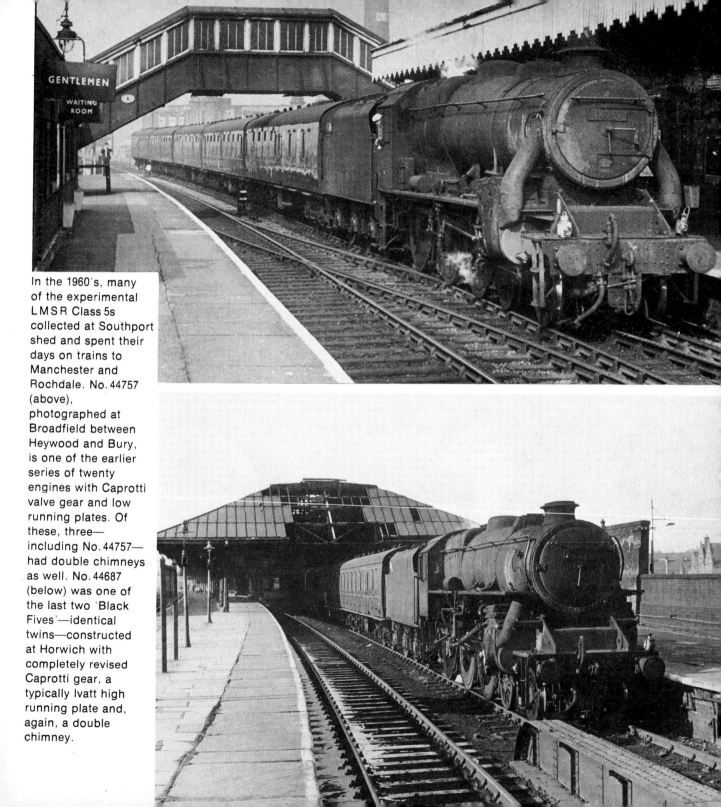

In the 1960's, many of the experimental LMSR Class 5s collected at Southport shed and spent their days on trains to Manchester and Rochdale. No. 44757 (above), photographed at Broadfield between Heywood and Bury, is one of the earlier series of twenty engines with Caprotti valve gear and low running plates. Of these, three—including No. 44757—had double chimneys as well. No. 44687 (below) was one of the last two 'Black Fives'—identical twins—constructed at Horwich with completely revised Caprotti gear, a typically Ivatt high running plate and, again, a double chimney.

Sound and fury from a Class 4 2-6-4T and a 'Black Five' climbing away from Cherry Tree Junction, Blackburn, towards Chorley with an excursion bound for Llandudno. From Chorley the train will take the L N W R line to Wigan via White Bear. Four miles of hard climbing, mostly at 1 in 60, face this train before it attains the summit at Brinscall.

Railway chronicler E. L. Ahrons once remarked that if you got lost on the L & Y, it would not matter as you would be bound to end up sooner or later at either Low Moor or Blackburn. Seven routes converged at the latter place—from Padiham, Accrington, Bolton, Chorley, Liverpool, Preston and Hellifield. Just backing onto its train at Blackburn ready to work the 10.19 a.m. to Hellifield in May 1961 is 4F 0-6-0 No. 44460.

Faced with mounting costs, the Midland Railway would have been happy to abandon their Settle–Carlisle extension, but the L & Y, eager for an alternative route to Scotland instead of having to rely on the L N W R, forced the Midland to complete the project. Trains to Scotland from both Manchester and Liverpool were routed via Hellifield onto the 'Long Drag'. Standard Class 4 No. 75048, of Bank Hall shed, climbs Whalley bank in the 1950's with a Hellifield–Blackburn train.

A midsummer scene at Wilpshire recalls days long past, as L & Y 'A' Class No. 52447 ambles through with a long freight. Note the poster advertising 'Day Returns' to Blackburn at eight old pence. As the old LMS signs dumped on the platform at the extreme right proclaim, Wilpshire was the station for the Roman camp of Ribchester.

Accrington station was not the most ideal for operating convenience. The tracks in the left foreground are those of the original East Lancashire Railway main line, the original platform in the immediate foreground being extremely low. Equally sharply-curved are the tracks towards Preston, where rebuilt 'Patriot' No. 45527 *Southport* stands with a Bank Holiday excursion from Blackpool to York on Whit Monday 1963. Note how, due to the curve, the end of the train can be seen on the extreme right of the picture. Passengers bound for the coast crowd on the opposite platform. Only the L & Y could have indulged in slipping coaches for such a station—which had to be done at the foot of the long 1 in 40 bank from Baxenden.

In this photograph from the other end of the station, No. 45216 as it enters the station with a Colne–Blackpool train is on the track adjacent to No. 45527 (seen on the previous page). The d.m.u. visible through the pillars is on the Manchester line, one of those in the foreground of the earlier photograph.

The Scotswood Sidings (Newcastle)–Red Bank (Manchester) ECS train was formed of the empty vans off two overnight newspaper trains from Manchester to the North East, Manchester being the principal newspaper printing centre in the provinces. When post-War austerity controls on the size of papers were eased in the mid-1950's this train increased enormously in length and thereafter was regularly doubleheaded. Many and varied combinations of motive power were used over the years but a rebuilt 'Royal Scot' No. 46117 *Welsh Guardsman*, piloting a 'Black Five' on 18 July 1961, seen at Sowerby Bridge, was a rarity.

'Britannia' Pacifics from Carlisle (Kingmoor) were regular performers on the train on Saturdays and Sundays in 1966, making a welcome relief from the ubiquitous Class 5s; No. 70011 *Hotspur* pilots No. 44947 one afternoon in May with the train nearing Middleton Junction.

Blackpool Illuminations in the autumn were a source of many excursions from far and wide. On Sunday 8 September 1963 'Britannia' No. 70039 *Sir Christopher Wren*, of Immingham shed, approaches Sowerby Bridge with an excursion from Scunthorpe bound for the 'Golden Mile'.

From numerous places nearer to Blackpool than the East Coast one could catch an Evening Excursion to see the Illuminations: Class 2P 4-4-0 No. 40584 takes water on Salwick troughs in September 1953 with a train from Accrington.

After diesels took over the workings on the Settle–Carlisle line, Holbeck's 'Jubilees' formed a pool of engines for excursion working. No. 45739 *Ulster* works hard to recover from the Charlestown slack as it passes Dover Bridge signalbox, between Hebden Bridge and Todmorden, in the summer of 1964.

As recently as 1966 there was a regular Illuminations train on Sunday afternoons from Blackpool to Leeds, the return working from a Friday evening outward trip. For the latter part of its route, from Manchester to Leeds, the train was scheduled over the LNW Diggle route. No. 45562 *Alberta* passes Blackrod station, junction for the branch to Horwich, on 2 October in that year.

Summer always brought an acute shortage of passenger engines and even the 'WD' 2-8-0s were pressed into passenger service when necessary. No. 90650 sets out from Sowerby Bridge with the Leeds portion of a Sunday excursion from Blackpool to Bradford and Leeds on 10 August 1958.